Co**r**

MW01122885

Written by Susan Griffiths

Illustrated by Peter Townsend

Contents   Page

Nelson
an International Thomson Publishing company I(T)P®

Oak Tree
Controversy

With these characters ...

Mr Rajiv

Mrs Ridge

Mayor Campbell

"Everyo

Setting the scene ...

Ten historic oak trees, planted by the first settlers in Oakville, will need to be cut down if the new supermarket is to be built. The mayor of Oakville tries hard to keep control of an angry town meeting, where the fate of the oak trees will be decided in a debate. But people from both sides feel very strongly about the issue, and no-one is interested in changing their minds. Everyone will hear the arguments for and against building the supermarket and then take a vote. But which side will win?

hought that they were right."

Chapter 1.

Mayor Campbell raised her heavy wooden hammer, and brought it down sharply on her bench. As she peered through her small glasses, the groups of angry people in the town hall fell silent. A difficult decision needed to be made at this meeting.

"It is now eight o'clock, so I call this meeting of the Oakville community to order," she said in a firm voice. "During tonight's debate, we will hear the arguments for and against building a new supermarket in the centre of our town."

The mayor looked around at all the people gathered in the town hall.

"There are people here who are for the new supermarket," she stated. "And there are people here who do not want the new supermarket built, because there are ten historic oak trees growing where it is planned to be built. This is a difficult issue to discuss. We must follow some rules for our meeting, so that everyone has a chance to present their point of view."

Everyone in the town hall listened politely, but they didn't really care about what the opposing group thought. Everyone thought that *they* were right. Each group had researched their argument thoroughly. They had also brought along objects supporting their presentation.

A table on one side of the hall was covered in leaves, acorns, old portrait photographs and a small antique spade.

On the other side of the hall was a trolley of groceries and a model of the supermarket building.

"Firstly, each side will have a chance to present its argument," continued Mayor Campbell. "As chairperson of the meeting, I will decide who can speak and when they can speak. Secondly, no-one is allowed to interrupt a person who is speaking. Does everyone understand the rules?"

There was a murmur of agreement from the large crowd of residents. The mayor smiled, but she felt worried. Everyone felt strongly about the issue. What was she going to do if the meeting got out of control?

"Right, now let's get started," she said loudly. "First, we will hear from the people who want the new supermarket to be built," said the mayor. "Who represents the supermarket owners?"

On the left-hand side of the town hall, in the front row, a tall man in a suit stood up.

"I do," said the man confidently.

The people on the right-hand side of the town hall whispered and grumbled and shuffled their feet. The people on the left-hand side of the town hall sat up straight and ignored them.

"Please tell us your name and your title," asked the mayor.

"My name is Mr Rajiv, and I will be the manager of the new supermarket," replied the man.

"Thank you," said the mayor. "Now, Mr Rajiv, please tell us why we should agree to build the new supermarket where the old oak trees stand." She started to take notes.

Chapter 2.

Mr Rajiv nodded politely to the mayor and turned to speak to the residents on the right-hand side of the hall.

"Madam Mayor and residents of Oakville, I understand why some people are against the new supermarket. We want to build it on a block of land where there are ten old, historic oak trees. We will need to cut them down to build our supermarket, and that's a shame. But there are three main reasons why we should be allowed to build our supermarket."

Mr Rajiv looked at his notes. He wanted to make sure that he gave an accurate explanation of his reasons. He hoped that the people on the right-hand side of the hall would change their minds. The people on the right-hand side frowned at Mr Rajiv.

"Reason number one: our research shows that there are many people in our town who need a supermarket close by. It's a long way to travel to the supermarket in the next town. Many older people can't travel there. We will have products in our supermarket that you can't buy in our town, and that will save people a lot of travelling time." Mr Rajiv held up some groceries from the trolley. "Our prices will also be much lower than the prices of other shops in Oakville, so everybody will save money."

Half of the people in the town hall nodded and the other half frowned, while shaking their heads. Mr Rajiv continued.

"Reason number two is that we will be able to offer people many jobs to build our supermarket. We can offer jobs to Oakville's builders, plumbers, electricians and painters." He pointed to the model building and smiled proudly. "The new supermarket was designed by the best architect in the country. It cleverly combines modern design with elegant, old-style features!"

"Once our supermarket is built, there will be jobs for many other people in Oakville. Some jobs will be full-time, for people who want to work all day. Others will be for people, like mums and dads, who want to work while their children are at school. Finally, there will be jobs for older students who want to work after school," explained Mr Rajiv, counting the types of jobs on his fingers.

"Reason number three is that our modern, new supermarket will encourage more people to shop in the centre of our town. By encouraging more people to come into the centre of town, it will mean that the other shops will become busier, too. The shopkeepers will have more customers, and they may be able to offer more jobs for people, too." Mr Rajiv held up his hands proudly to show how many types of jobs would be created.

At that moment, Mr Rajiv was rudely interrupted.

"Who wants to come to a town centre that has only concrete buildings and too much traffic?" asked a woman from the right-hand side of the town hall. "I certainly don't!" she said, as she raised her arms, looking very upset. "What sort of town wants huge delivery trucks and shopping trolleys clogging up their streets? People want beautiful trees that have taken a hundred years to grow!"

The mayor banged her wooden hammer heavily on the bench, but the woman ignored her.

"My great-grandfather was one of the people who planted those oak trees!" exclaimed the woman angrily. She sat down, and the people on the right-hand side of the hall clapped loudly.

"Order! Order!" fumed the mayor, banging her hammer again. "Your side will have its turn but, until then, you really must be quiet!" She waved at Mr Rajiv to continue.

"In summary, if we are allowed to build our supermarket, our town will lose historic old oak trees. But we will gain many benefits. We will have easier shopping, lower prices, more jobs and happy shopkeepers. This stunning supermarket will put Oakville on the map! We think that these benefits are more important than keeping old oak trees," said Mr Rajiv.

Mr Rajiv sat down, and the people on the left-hand side of the town hall clapped loudly. The other half folded their arms, looking unimpressed. They did not agree with anything Mr Rajiv had said. They waited impatiently for the mayor to finish writing her notes and call on their speaker.

"Thank you, Mr Rajiv," said the mayor. "Now, we will hear from the side who want to save the historic old oak trees. Who represents the people against the supermarket?"

On the right-hand side of the town hall, in the front row, the woman who had interrupted Mr Rajiv stood up. The mayor frowned at the woman over her small glasses.

"I do," said the woman.

"Please state your name and your title," asked the mayor.

"My name is Mrs Ridge, spokes-person for the Oakville conservation group," she replied.

"Very well," said the mayor. "Please tell us why your group is against building the new supermarket in the town centre."

Chapter 3.

Mrs Ridge turned to speak to the residents in the town hall. The people on the left-hand side of the town hall looked bored. They disrespectfully whispered amongst each other and yawned.

The people on the right-hand side were all listening carefully and nodding as Mrs Ridge spoke.

"Our conservation group has three very important reasons for wanting to preserve our historic oak trees," said Mrs Ridge boldly.

"The first reason is that they remind us of our ancestors. When our town was founded, over a hundred years ago, the people who settled here faced many hardships. The land was not good for farming, and many of their crops failed. Many people became sick, because they did not have clean water or enough good food. As if that wasn't tough enough, a great fire swept through the town destroying many homes."

Mrs Ridge pointed at the old portrait photographs on the table.

"Despite these disasters, our ancestors, who came from many different countries and cultures, were determined to make a new life for themselves. Slowly, they learned how to farm the land. They discovered clean water trickling from a spring in the hills. They rebuilt their houses from stone, instead of wood. They refused to give up."

"When the worst of those early years was over, they decided that it was important to have a memorial. This memorial would remind people in the future of how hard those early settlers worked to turn this place into a town where people wanted to live."

Mrs Ridge picked up an acorn. "Instead of building a stone or metal monument, they planted oak trees as a *living* memorial."

"They hoped that, in years to come, people would look at their trees, remember the settlers and think about how lucky they were now. That memorial is what the supermarket owners don't respect and want to cut down. If we lose the trees, we also lose part of our history and our heritage. That would be something we could never replace. It would be very disrespectful to our early settlers." Mrs Ridge looked around the hall. Her supporters mumbled in agreement.

"The second reason we want to save the trees, is that our town centre has grown so much in the last hundred years that there are hardly any parks or trees left. We are already surrounded by too many tall buildings, shops and houses. And *our* research shows that people want to preserve the trees that remain. They want places where they can rest and relax."

"The old oak trees provide a place where people can sit, and children and pets can play safely. Under those wide, spreading branches, people can have picnics and enjoy some peace and quiet."

"If we lose our trees, we will have nothing but concrete and glass and metal surrounding us," continued Mrs Ridge.

"The third reason is that the old oak trees provide homes to many animals, such as birds, lizards and insects, that will have nowhere else to live if they are cut down. We people must share our town with other living things. If there is nowhere for them to live, they will disappear."

"Excuse me! If I don't have a job, how will my family and I be able to live?" interrupted a woman angrily from the left-hand side of the town hall. "I will certainly have no money for picnics!" There was a murmur of approval from the people surrounding her.

Once more, Mayor Campbell banged her hammer on the bench.

"Order!" she said, looking sternly at the woman. "I will not allow any more interruptions!"

The woman sat down grumpily, and the people on the left-hand side of the town hall grumbled quietly, and then fell silent. Mrs Ridge continued.

"The old oak trees provide a safe environment for all sorts of living things that depend upon each other and the trees for their survival. It is important that we conserve some natural places for our animals, birds and other plants. Our lives will seem terribly empty if all we can see and hear are cars and trucks, rather than small animals playing in the branches and birds singing in the tree-tops."

Mrs Ridge sat down, and the people around her clapped loudly.

"Well done!" they said. Everyone on the right-hand side of the hall believed that their reasons were far more important than anything that Mr Rajiv had presented at the meeting.

The mayor banged her hammer once more, and waited for the people in the town hall to become quiet again.

Chapter 4

"During the debate, we heard arguments for and against the new supermarket. This really is a difficult issue," said the mayor firmly.

"Both sides presented very good arguments. Now," she said, looking around the town hall, "we will have a vote."

People who worked for the city council handed out voting forms. Two choices were listed: to preserve the oak trees, or to allow the supermarket to be built. Everyone ticked their choice on the form. The council workers collected the forms when everyone had finished voting.

Mayor Campbell stood up and strode into her office to supervise the vote counting.

Everyone in the town hall stood up, too, and started talking noisily. The people on the side of the supermarket thought that they had won. The people on the side of the trees thought that they had won. For thirty minutes, arguments between people from both sides raged throughout the hall, as people discussed what had been said during the debate.

Suddenly, everyone became silent as the door to the mayor's office swung open. Mayor Campbell strode towards her bench. Everyone in the town hall sat down again, and waited anxiously for the result. Who had won the vote? What would happen? Would the trees be saved? Would the supermarket be built? Everyone held their breath as the mayor sat down and banged her hammer once more.

"I call this meeting to order again," she said. "The results of the voting are as follows." She put her glasses on and read the results. "The total votes for building the supermarket: 120."

The people on the left-hand side of the town hall cheered. That sounded like enough votes to win!

"And the total votes for preserving the trees ..." The mayor looked up at the crowd. "120."

Everyone in the town hall groaned. It was a tie. The issue would have to be decided by the mayor.

The mayor continued. "Even though it was not easy, I have had to make the final decision myself."

Everyone fell silent and sat forward on the edge of their seats. Mr Rajiv nervously rubbed his chin. Mrs Ridge anxiously fiddled with her earring. Mayor Campbell picked up a piece of paper and started to read out her decision.

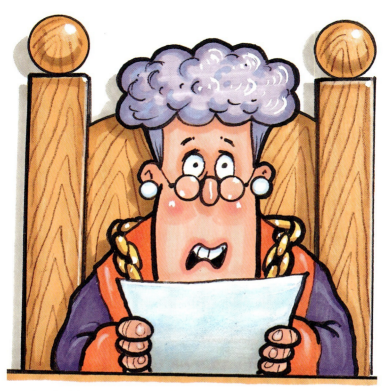

Half the people in the town hall smiled and cheered and clapped. The other half looked very upset, and grouched and grizzled loudly. But which half? The people on the left-hand side or the right-hand side?

You decide.

"Order! Order!"

Oaks
Green, shady
Rustling, living, growing
Leaves, branches, windows, carparks
Bustling, queuing, shopping
Bright, new
Supermarket.